You Can't Beat God Givin'

Miracle Testimonies From Ordinary People Serving an Extraordinary God

You Can't Beat God Givin'

Miracle Testimonies From Ordinary People
Serving an Extraordinary God

by
R. W. Schambach

POWER PUBLICATIONS • TYLER, TEXAS

All Scripture quotations are taken from the *King James Version* of the Bible.

You Can't Beat God Givin'—
Miracle Testimonies From Ordinary People
Serving an Extraordinary God
ISBN O-89274-690-4
Copyright © 1994 by R. W. Schambach
P. O. Box 9009
Tyler, Texas 75711

Contents

1 Our Nothing Is Something to God   7

2 Twenty-six Miracles   15

3 The $10,000 Bribe   23

4 The $100 Car   25

5 The $100 House   27

6 The $600 Tent   33

7 "But, Lord!"   35

8 Brother Thompson's Miracle   37

9 "Old Red"   39

10 That's My Cow in There   43

11 Giving in Haiti   47

12 Giving to God, Not to Man   51

13 God Provides Food   53

14 Multiplying Money   55

15 My Mom, the Bank   57

16 New Car Deal   61

17 Building in Newark   63

18 Obedience Pays Off   69

19 Power Partner Pennaman   71

20 Pray Specifically   73

21 My $100 Pledge   75

22 My Used Truck Lot   79

23 Tithing Opens Blind Eyes   83

24 Giving in Trinidad   85

25 Beer Business Tithes?   87

26 Fertile Ground   89

1
Our Nothing Is Something to God

God is the best giver in the world. That's what this book is going to show you: how God continually gives to those who obey Him, because you can't beat God giving! I remember the sawdust on the ground at the old tent services and the mamas and the little grandmas who would march up the trail to the altar with their offerings to God, singing:

You can't beat God givin',

no matter how you try

You can't beat God givin';

no matter how you try

The more you give,

the more He gives you.

Just keep on givin'

— because it's really true —

You can't beat God givin',

no matter how you try.

But, you know, these are more than just the words to a beautiful song. This is a tried and true principle of God's Word. The people you are going to read about in this book are people just like you and me, people who heard the voice of God, obeyed Him and were richly blessed for it. They are people like the little widow of Zarephath in 1 Kings 17:8. Do you remember her story?

God was angry at the wickedness of the people of Israel because their queen, Jezebel, had made Baal the idol in their land. God had anointed Elijah and told him to let Jezebel know there was going to be a great famine in their land because she wouldn't repent and lead the people back to God. The famine started, and it was terrible: no rain, dead crops. People began to starve to death. It was all right for Elijah for a little while because God led him to a nice babbling brook where he could relax all day and every evening eat food God sent ravens to give him. But one day that brook dried up because there wasn't any rain. The ravens were more than a little late coming that day. They didn't show up at all. But God told Elijah, "That's all right. I have a plan for you. Go over to Zarephath; I have a widow lady there who's going to take care of you."

This idea probably didn't seem too good to Elijah. In the first place, Queen Jezebel wasn't too happy with him right then; in fact, she was looking everywhere for him because she figured he was responsible for the famine that was ruining their land. And Zarephath was the queen's hometown. God might as well have been saying, "Put your head in the lion's mouth." In the second place, widow ladies in Bible times weren't known for having a lot of means to support starving prophets. If a widow didn't have a grown-up son to provide for her, she was pretty likely to starve to death — especially in the middle of a famine!

But Elijah did what God commanded. Look in
1 Kings 17.

And the word of the Lord came unto him, saying,

Arise, get thee to Zarephath, which belongeth to
Zidon, and dwell there: behold, I have commanded a
widow woman there to sustain thee.

So he arose and went to Zarephath. And when he
came to the gate of the city, behold, the widow woman
was there gathering of sticks: and he called to her, and
said, Fetch me, I pray thee, a little water in a vessel, that I
may drink.

And as she was going to fetch it, he called to her, and
said, Bring me, I pray thee, a morsel of bread in thine
hand.

And she said, As the Lord thy God liveth, I have not a
cake, but an handful of meal in a barrel, and a little oil in
a cruse: and, behold, I am gathering two sticks, that I may
go in and dress it for me and my son, that we may eat it,
and die.

And Elijah said unto her, Fear not; go and do as thou
hast said: but make me thereof a little cake first, and
bring it unto me, and after make for thee and for thy son.

For thus saith the Lord God of Israel, The barrel of
meal shall not waste, neither shall the cruse of oil fail,
until the day that the Lord sendeth rain upon the earth.

And she went and did according to the saying of
Elijah: and she, and he, and her house, did eat many
days.

And the barrel of meal wasted not, neither did the
cruse of oil fail, according to the word of the Lord, which
he spake by Elijah.

1 Kings 17: 8-16

Can you see this picture? When the prophet came to
the gates of Zarephath, he saw a skinny, broken-down
little widow woman picking up sticks. "Praise the

Lord, sister," he said to her. "I sure am thirsty. Will you go get me a drink?"

She said, "Praise the Lord, brother. I'll get you a drink right now."

But then Elijah said, "Wait a minute. Will you bring me a morsel of bread, too?"

This little lady, with a stricken look on her face, told the prophet, "As the Lord liveth, I don't have any bread. Haven't you heard about the famine?' (If only she knew he was the rascal who caused the famine!) "I'm down to my *last* cake, and I'm out here picking up sticks for the *last* time. I'm going to mix the meal for the *last* time and strike the fire for the *last* time; then, my son and I are going to sit down to a meal together for the *last* time."

Everything was last, last, last. This lady thought this was her last day on earth because she and her boy were going to starve to death after they finished this little bit of meal.

How do you think this made Elijah feel knowing that God thought this starving little widow was going to take care of him?

But I'll let you in on a secret: God doesn't look at things the same way we do. What looks like nothing to us is something to God. God is the Creator. He can make something out of our nothing. That's why many times, when you are waiting for God to do something in your life — to give you something or to change a situation in your life, when you need a real touch from Him — He just waits. He waits until you are down to "nothing"; because that's exactly when God can do His biggest miracles — God can do something great with your "nothing." But it takes obedience to clear the way for God to do a miracle!

I know a lot of preachers who pray, "Lord, just send a millionaire to my church. Send me a millionaire." But that's probably not going to happen. Elijah might have been praying, "Lord, make this widow lady of Zarephath a very rich widow"; but, no, God sent Elijah to a little lady who was about to starve to death. God doesn't need to work through millionaires and rich widows; He can work through people like that little lady of Zarephath.

That little widow didn't have enough food to feed a hungry prophet like Elijah; she had her own child to feed. But Elijah told her, "You go do just what you said — make that last bit of bread — but give it to me, then feed you and your son." (You see, preachers have always had a lot of nerve, even back in Bible times.) Elijah, who had been waiting on ravens to bring him food, had a lot of nerve asking this woman to give him her last meal.

But that widow lady knew Elijah was a man of God, and God had already spoken to her and told her to step out on faith and give what she had to the man of God.

If God speaks to you, He expects you to listen. Even if you're down to your very last dollar, if God says to give it to His Church, you had better listen. He doesn't ask you to give something unless He has something bigger and better planned for you.

The widow of Zarephath went in and mixed up her last little cake and gave it to Elijah. Then she mixed up a cake for her son and a cake for her. And the Bible says there was more meal and more oil, and that the meal barrel wasted not for more than 1,000 days. That's over three years! For three years that lady had a perpetual miracle right in her home because she obeyed the voice of God.

I can just hear her, "Brother, you can stay right here with me in Zarephath. You don't need to go down the street to Sister Jones' house. She hasn't got a thing to eat down there. You stay here, and I'll take care of you." And for three years, until that famine ended, they ate and drank and were fine in her house.

Now, a lot of people say to me, "Brother Schambach, these are the worst economic times I can remember in years. I can barely make the house payment, and I just can't afford to give an offering until things start looking up. I haven't even been tithing."

And I always say to those people, "You are making the biggest mistake that you could possibly make. A time of calamity, a time of poverty, or a time of disaster is the very worst time to stop giving. Can you think of a worse calamity than the one facing the little widow of Zarephath? She and her son had been surviving by sharing one little cake every day, until finally they were down to the very last cake. She had no business at all giving that cake to someone else! That was the very worst day of her life. She had nothing to share. But what would have happened to her and her son if she had told the man of God, "You know, I just can't afford to give until things start looking up"? Both she and her boy would have perished. Instead, because she was obedient and gave even in the midst of terrible need, she received a perpetual miracle of abundant food for three years.

All around her was famine; thousands of people were starving to death, but because Elijah and the widow obeyed God, the famine did not touch them at all. So, although there may be difficult economic times, and all around you people may be in dire circumstances, God is not going to let that touch you if you are obedient to Him.

Here is a promise from God for you:

> **Thou shalt not be afraid for the terror by night; nor for the arrow that flieth by day;**
>
> **Nor for the pestilence that walketh in darkness; nor for the destruction that wasteth at noonday.**
>
> **A thousand shall fall at thy side, and ten thousand at thy right hand; but it shall not come nigh thee.**
>
> **Psalm 91:5-7**

You don't have to worry about the recession or the economy. Whatever is happening to the rest of the world doesn't have to touch you. All you have to do is obey the voice of God.

There was a famine in the land, and all the widow's neighbors were starving and dying, but she didn't pay attention to that; she simply took God at His Word. She gave one little meal cake, and God gave back to her a thousand times over what she had given. You just can't beat God giving!

I'm not saying that if you give your last dollar today to God's work that you're going to get rich, because I don't believe God makes petty deals like that. But I will tell you this: *God honors our giving.*

We have God's promise.

> **But this I say, He which soweth sparingly shall reap also sparingly; and he which soweth bountifully shall reap also bountifully.**
>
> **Every man according as he purposeth in his heart, so let him give; not grudgingly, or of necessity: for God loveth a cheerful giver.**
>
> **And God is able to make all grace abound toward you; that ye, always having all sufficiency in all things, may abound to every good work.**
>
> 2 Corinthians 9:6-8

In my work and ministry, I have met hundreds of people and heard hundreds of stories of God's children obeying His voice and receiving in return the very desires of their heart. You're going to meet some of those people in the pages of this book, and I know that it is going to bless and inspire you.

I hope by the time you finish reading this book that you are convinced that you can't beat God giving — no matter how you try. And I trust that as you read these stories and marvel at the grace of God that your spirit will be open to sow the seed God has given you into His fertile fields. You see, a lot of people eat their seed instead of sowing it. But what happens then? If you eat your seed, it's gone; but if you sow that seed, instead, it sprouts and grows and returns a harvest to you. So, keep reading and meet some people who sowed their seed into fertile ground and who were blessed by the greatest Giver of Gifts!

2
Twenty-six Miracles

When I was on the Phil Donahue show he asked me, "What is the greatest miracle you have ever seen?"

Of course, I told him the greatest miracle is that Jesus reaches down into the depths of sin, picks up a man and washes him in His blood, clothes him with His righteousness and writes his name in the Lamb's book of life. That is the greatest miracle.

But what Phil wanted to know was what kind of healing or supernatural occurrence in the everyday world was the most dramatic move of God I have ever seen. And I have seen so many.

Back in 1957, Gene Mullinex, from Little Rock, Arkansas, had a lung that had been diagnosed with tuberculosis. It had to be removed, and, in order to get to it, three of his ribs had to be removed. After that operation, he was left with a hole in his back. When he came into our meeting, we laid hands on him, prayed with him, and God gave him a brand new lung and three replacement ribs and healed that hole in his back.

I remember a precious little lady from St. Louis, Missouri, who was a hopeless cripple in a wheelchair. She was instantaneously healed when we prayed for her. To this day, she keeps her medical records. Her doctor wrote the word "miracle" across his report.

A man from West Virginia lost both his eyes in a coal mining accident. We laid hands on him and prayed for him. When we drew our hands away, God had placed two brand new brown eyes in the sockets. God performs creative miracles!

A lady in Chicago, Illinois, lost her foot because of gangrene. But God began a work on that woman, and her foot started to grow back. After four months' time, she had a new foot with new toes on it!

Then again, often times, I have seen miracles come as a result of a sacrificial offering. That doesn't mean we can buy a healing; but we can show faith with an offering and God will take that faith and use it to meet our need. I'll never forget, the greatest miracle I ever witnessed began with an offering. It happened under the ministry of Brother A. A. Allen. I was with this man of God for about five years in the fifties. When this great miracle happened, Dr. John Douglas (perhaps you have heard him on the radio) and Brother Allen were together. I believe it was one of the greatest evangelistic teams of that day. A woman brought her child, who had twenty-six major diseases, to our meeting. I'll never forget this as long as I live. The boy was born blind, deaf and mute. Both arms were crippled and deformed. His elbows protruded up into his little tummy; his knees touched his elbows. Both legs were crippled and deformed; he had club feet. When he was born, his doctors said that boy would never live to see his first birthday, but they were wrong; he was approaching four years of age. Of course, his condition was breaking his mama's heart. She came to our meetings all week, and I got concerned about that boy. In those crusades, we had each person with a need fill out a prayer card, and as the Holy Spirit moved, we would pray for the needs God inspired us to pray for. And the Holy Spirit didn't seem to be moving us to pray for that little boy.

The following Sunday, his mother came to me and said, "Brother Schambach, I'm down to my last twenty dollars. I've paid the hotel bill, but we've been eating in the restaurant, coming to three services a day and giving in every offering. All the money has run out. My baby has not been prayed for." She was very upset, and she was ready to give up and go home.

I said, "Ma'am, I can't apologize for the moving of the Holy Ghost. I know you have to leave tonight, but if you come to the service and, once again, the Holy Spirit leads in another direction, and your son's prayer card is not drawn for prayer, I will personally take your baby to the man of God's trailer house and see that he lays hands on your baby. You will not leave disappointed." And I meant that from my heart.

That night I came out, and I led the singing in that evening service. Then I introduced Brother A. A. Allen, and he came bouncing out on that platform and said, "Tonight we're going to receive an offering of faith." I had never heard him use that expression before, and I saw eyebrows lift all over the congregation. He went on, "Now, if you don't know what I mean when I say an 'offering of faith,' I mean for you to give God something you cannot afford to give. That's a good definition, isn't it? If you can afford it, there's no faith connected to it. So give Him something you can't afford to give."

As soon as Brother Allen said that, I saw that boy's mother leap out into the aisle and come running. Three thousand people were watching her in that Birmingham Fairgrounds Arena as she threw something in that offering bucket. I never saw anybody in such a hurry to give, and, I confess, I was nosy. I came down off that platform to see what she had given. You know what I saw in that bucket? A twenty dollar bill.

I knew that was all she had. She had told me that. She had driven from Knoxville, Tennessee, to the meeting in Birmingham, Alabama. She didn't know how she was going to get home or what she was going to use to feed herself and her baby on the way. I went behind that platform and wept. I prayed, "Lord, I've been trying to teach that woman faith all week. But now I'm asking You to give me faith like she's got!"

I don't know whether I could have done what she did, and you don't know if you could do it. We will never know, unless we are in a similar situation. But Brother Allen went on and collected the offering and launched into his sermon. But about fifteen minutes into his message he stopped and said, "I'm being carried away in the Spirit."

I said to myself, "Here we go again on another trip." This is how God used him: he said he could see what the Holy Spirit wanted to communicate to him like he was watching it on a television screen. He would describe it as he saw it. That night he said, "I'm being carried away to a huge white building. Oh, it's a hospital." Of course, I heard this kind of thing every night that I worked with Brother Allen so I was sitting there unmoved.

Then he said, "I'm inside the hospital, and there's no doubt in my mind where I'm heading because I hear all these babies crying. It's a maternity ward. I see five doctors around a table. A little baby has been born. The baby was born with twelve, no, sixteen, no, twenty-six diseases."

When he said that, I started getting chill bumps up and down my spine. I said, "Oh, my God, tonight's that baby's night!"

Brother Allen continued, "Twenty-six diseases. The doctors said he'd never live to see his first birthday, but that's not so. That boy is approaching four. Now I see the mother packing a suitcase. They're going on a trip. Another lady's with her. The baby's in a bassinet. It's in the back seat of an old Ford. They're driving down the highway. I see the Alabama/Tennessee border. That automobile is driving in the parking lot. Lady, you're here tonight. Bring me that baby! God's going to give you twenty-six miracles."

That woman came running again for the second time that night. She put the baby in Brother Allen's arms. I jumped up to stand beside him, and everybody in the audience — 3,000 strong — was standing. Brother Allen must have wanted to be sure that the audience was agreeing in faith for the miracle because he said, "Everybody, close your eyes." But I thought, *Not me, mister. I'm going to be scriptural on this one. I'm going to watch and pray. I've been waiting for this all week.*

That little boy's tongue had been hanging out of his mouth all week. The first thing I saw as Brother Allen prayed was that tongue snap back in the mouth like a rubber band. For the first time in four years, the little guy's tongue was in his mouth. I saw two little whirlpools in his eyes, just a milky color. You couldn't tell whether he had blue or brown or what color of eyes. But during the prayer, that whirlpool ceased, and I saw two brand new brown eyes! I knew God had opened his eyes, and if God opened the eyes, I knew He had unstopped the deaf ears.

Then those little arms began to snap like pieces of wood; and for the first time, they stretched out. The legs cracked like wood popping. All of a sudden, I saw God form toes out of those club feet as easily as a child forms something with silly-putty. The crowd was watching by this time going wild! I've never seen any people shout and rejoice so much in all my life.

I saw that baby placed on his feet, and he began to run for the first time in his life. He had never seen his mama before, never said a word, but he began running across the platform — and I was running right after him trying to catch him. He leaped into his mama's arms, and I heard him say his first word, "Mama."

This miracle charged up the people of God so much that even more miracles began to happen there in Birmingham. We stayed for a week after that. People were bringing their handicapped friends and family members. There were about twelve or thirteen people in wheelchairs over against one wall on the left side of the platform, and about fifteen or so people who had been brought from the local hospital on stretchers on the right side of the platform. When everybody saw the power of God at work, all the handicapped people in wheelchairs stood up like a platoon of soldiers and walked out of there healed by the power of God, without hands ever being laid on them. Then 3,000 pairs of eyes, like they were being conducted by a conductor, looked in anticipation from the wheelchairs to the stretchers. The next thing you knew, everybody on the stretchers got up and walked out of there healed by the power of God! Six blind people in the audience came running down the aisle with their white canes and threw them on the platform. Their eyes had been opened! Hearing aids began to pile up, then canes and crutches. Everybody in the building was healed.

It was an incredible time of miracles, and the power of God fell, starting with the twenty-six miracles for that one little boy. The following Saturday after his healing, I received a special delivery letter from his mother. She knew that I had a soft spot in my heart for her little son, so she wrote me. She said, "Brother Schambach, I took the baby to the hospital Monday morning, and the doctors won't give him back. They have kept him all week. They have called in every doctor from all over the country who has had anything to do with the case. They have pronounced my baby cured of twenty-six major diseases." Of course, we went on to get the copies of the affidavits from the doctors certifying that boy's life was a genuine miracle.

But there was a P.S. in that dear lady's letter, and a P.S. always means there's something more to the story. Her letter continued, "You remember that last Sunday when I told you all I had was twenty dollars? God knows that was the truth. But when that man of God said to give something you can't afford, I leaped into the aisle. The moment I hit that aisle, for the first time in my life, I heard the devil talk. The devil told me, 'You can't give that; that's not yours. Fifteen dollars of that goes to the doctor. Five dollars is for gas to get home.' The faster I ran, the faster he talked. But as soon as I turned loose of that money, he stopped talking. Ain't no use talking now. It's gone! It's been put in the bucket now.

"Brother Schambach, all you saw was those twenty-six miracles, but there is one you don't know anything about. After you were gone, people were staying there. They wanted to see the baby and see what God had done. People shook hands with me. When one lady shook my hands, I felt a folded piece of paper between our palms. I opened it up and saw it was a twenty dollar bill. As I shook hands with the people who had lined up, every one of them had a folded paper in their hand. I went into the ladies room and counted $235!

"Isn't that just like God? He not only gave me twenty-six miracles for my baby, but He allowed me to stay in a hotel for a week, pay my bills, eat three meals a day in restaurants, give in three offerings every day, and still go home with more money than I came with!"

You can't beat God giving, no matter how much you try. Hallelujah! I believe with all my heart, as a result of what I saw, that the miracle had its origin in that gift of faith. When God dealt with that woman, she gave her last, and her last became her first.

3
The $10,000 Bribe

In Sacramento, a man put a check in my hand and said, "Hey, preacher, this is yours."

I said, "Thank you."

He said, "It's yours if..."

In my heart I said, "Oh, no," because I knew he was going to put a string on the gift. "If what?"

He said, "If you can heal my daughter. She has epilepsy."

I said, "Do you mind if I look at this check...before I tear it up?" It was a $10,000 check. I tore that thing up and put it back in his hand. "Who do you think you are?" I asked him. "You think that just because you can write a check like this that you can buy something from God? You've got to receive from God on the same level as the poor man. You've got to believe God if you're going to have a miracle, mister."

Now, I didn't tell him this, but I believe if he would have put that check in the offering bucket, without making a scene, he could have moved God with the faith he showed by giving that sacrificial offering. You see, there's a way to give. Some people like to be seen; there's no blessing involved in that. But the Lord doesn't look at the size of the gift; He looks at the heart that gives and the sacrifice which has gone into the gift.

While we can move God with our *faith* in giving an offering, we cannot buy anything from God. If we try, our trust is in the money, not in God.

Do you remember the widow's mite in Luke 21?

> And he looked up, and saw the rich men casting their gifts into the treasury.
>
> And he saw also a certain poor widow casting in thither two mites.
>
> And he said, Of a truth I say unto you, that this poor widow hath cast in more than they all:
>
> For all these have of their abundance cast in unto the offerings of God: but she of her penury hath cast in all the living that she had."
>
> **Luke 21:1-4**

You can move God by your giving because your giving shows God your faith. Jesus noticed even the tiny gift of that widow, and He was moved. But in order to move God with a gift, you must give in faith, in humility and as a sacrifice. Don't expect God to be impressed by a $10,000 bribe.

4
The $100 Car

I had preached at Christ for the Nations — the school founded by Gordon and Freida Lindsay in Dallas, Texas — and almost a year later, I received a beautiful letter from one of the students.

The student wrote, "Brother Schambach, I was under your tent in Arlington, Texas, last year. You were receiving an offering, and you were asking people to pray about giving $100. That's all that I had. It was my car payment. *God* told me to give my car payment."

I don't ask folks to do that. I don't want anyone to give me money that they owe to somebody else — robbing Peter to pay Paul, as the saying goes. But when *God* tells you to do something, you had better do what He says.

The letter went on, "I gave that car payment, and I came to you and told you that. You took me by the hand and said, 'God's going to give you a brand new car.'" (I don't even remember saying that because I was under the anointing of the Holy Ghost.)

This boy continued in his letter, "You also said God was going to pay for my whole tuition for three years of Bible college. I want you to know that God blessed me with a new car and $19,000. A gift is on the way right now to your office in Tyler, Texas."

I started dancing when I read that: $19,000, and it all came from planting a seed of $100. You can't beat God giving!

5

The $100 House

Faith was high in Chicago; we were having a great meeting. I took almost a truckload of canes and crutches and wheelchairs out of that meeting. Faith was so high, in fact, that I challenged the 3,500 people in the audience, "I dare you to give God the biggest bill you've got."

I never heard so many groans in all my life. I had twenty-one preachers on the platform, and they were thinking, *Oh, Lord, I knew I should have changed that twenty dollar bill before I got to church.*

I believe it was one of the greatest offerings I ever received for God. Everybody accepted the challenge. There was one black preacher, a dear friend of mine, who came and stood behind me holding something in his hand. I put the bucket around to him and said, "Turn it loose, brother."

He said, "Man, you don't know what I've got."

I said, "What have you got?"

He said, "Man, I've got one of those $100 bills."

"It's going to take some faith to turn that thing loose," I told him.

He said, "Well, it ain't mine."

"What's it doing in your hand?" I asked.

"Well," he said, "I got caught speeding. I was fined $100. I was going to go pay that fine tomorrow."

I said, "Go pay the fine."

He said, "But I want the blessing!"

I said, "Turn it loose, then."

"What about the fine?"

I said, "Pay it."

"But I want to be blessed."

"You aren't putting me in the middle," I said. "Fight the devil yourself." Meanwhile, people were still coming, putting $20s and $10s in the offering. Finally he came and turned loose of that $100. He watched it float all the way to the bottom of the bucket.

I'll never forget this as long as I live. We continued our meetings for thirty days. They were tremendous meetings in that coliseum in Chicago. The very next night after I received that offering, I heard many testimonies of people who got blessed because they gave, because they had accepted the challenge.

One pastor said, "I had $6. I gave God the $5; I kept the $1. Today God blessed me with $167."

Another person said, "I gave twenty and got sixty back."

Another person said, "I gave $10 and got $400."

I went to my friend and said, "What did you get back?"

He said, "Nothing."

The second night more people testified. Once again, when I asked my friend what he had received, he said, "Nothing!" He was getting nervous now. The third night I didn't bother asking him; he had his head between his knees moaning, "Oh, Lord." I knew he hadn't received anything. The fourth night he wasn't even there. But on the fifth night, I was getting ready to preach when the back doors opened, and he bounced in. I saw something white in his hand. He had a white piece of paper and he hollered, "Schambach, I got it!"

Inside I was saying, "Lord, it's about time." But to him I said, "Come on, brother, tell us about it."

I didn't get to preach that night. He tore the place up with the story I'm telling you. He said, "This preacher taught me something: that God doesn't always return a blessing in twenty-four hours. Sometimes you have to wait on Him.

> **They that wait upon the Lord shall renew their strength; they shall mount up with wings as eagles; they shall run, and not be weary; and they shall walk, and not faint.**
>
> **Isaiah 40:31**

He went on, "I've been sitting here struggling the last few nights listening to you testify. I gave my best, too. You all got something back, and I was sitting there wondering what was wrong with me. I had given $100. This morning I got a telephone call from a Full Gospel Businessman in Chicago."

This Christian man had said, "Brother, can you be in my office at one o'clock today? I've got something for you."

My friend said, "Yes, sir, I sure can be there. But where is your office? I don't know who you are."

The businessman said, "Well, I don't know who you are, either, but you be here." So he gave my friend directions to his office.

At one o'clock in that man's office, the businessman said, "God has blessed me in this city over the past thirty years. Before I go to work in the morning, I always pray to get the direction of the Holy Spirit. This morning God told me to give you a house."

My friend stared at the man and said, "But I don't even know you."

The businessman said, "That's what I told God, 'I don't know the man.' God said, 'I do.' God has blessed me with a lot of property in this city, and He told me to give you the best house I have." He already had the deed made out to my friend. The deed was for a $50,000 home.

With tears running down his face, my friend told the business man, "My wife and I have been pastoring here for three years, living in one room with our three children. We've been on the verge of doubting the call of God: Did God really call us? If God called, why do we have to go through this? The other night I was in another preacher's meeting, down to my last $100, and that wasn't even mine. But God worked on me to turn that offering loose. How I thank God now that I turned it loose! I had to be reduced to nothing. But how did you find me, brother? I don't have a telephone listing; you don't know where I live."

The businessman said, "I know. I told the Lord that I didn't know how to get in touch with you; I didn't know where you lived. But God told me your telephone number. God gave me that number when I called you this morning and told you to come to my office."

When my friend finished telling the story, he put the deed to his house into my hand — I saw it; I read it. I was the first one he had shown it to. I would have loved to tell that story that night, but it was his story, and he told it with such joy!

Of course, that night, after the service, everyone wanted to give $100 and get a free house, but I turned around and rebuked them. I said, "Now that you saw somebody put it to work and get a blessing, you want to try it. It isn't going to work the same way for you. You've got to move when God moves or you will be moving on your own."

Do you remember when the children of Israel were at Kadesh-barnea? (See Numbers 13,14.) Two reports came back from the twelve spies sent to search out the Promised Land before the Israelites went in. The reports came back like this: ten spies said, "There's no way we can take this land," and two spies said, "Let's do it in God's name!"

The ten spies were so scared of going into that land, and they frightened the people so much, that the crowd picked up stones to kill Joshua and Caleb, the two faithful spies.

God was so angry about their failure to obey Him and enter into the land that He said, "I'm going to kill every one of them."

31

But Moses interceded and said, "Don't destroy them, Lord."

God said, "All right, Moses. I won't kill them, but turn them around. They're not going into the land I promised them."

But when the people heard that — and after they had a chance to sleep on it — they came to Moses the next day and said, "We changed our minds. We trust God after all. We want to go claim the land."

But God said, "No, they don't. If they go now, they're going on their own."

When God moves, when you feel the rustling of His Spirit, you had better move with Him or you'll move on your own!

6
The $600 Tent

One night during a tent revival, I told the folks, "I need 1,000 people across this nation who will give $100, and this tent will be paid for."

I saw a grown man dressed up nicely, and I could tell that he was a preacher. He was weeping, vehemently sobbing, heading right for me. He had six $100 bills in his hand. He put them in my hand. I said, "What are you crying for, brother?"

"Oh," he said, "I'm an evangelist, and I lost my tent. I've been saving this to buy a tent. And sitting there, God told me to give my tent savings to you!"

I knew what he was going through. But I also knew that when God tells you to make a step of faith, He has a plan and a reward in mind. I said, "Is that all He told you — just to give it?"

And this young evangelist said, "No, sir. He said if I gave it, He was going to give me a tent."

I said, "Then dry the tears up, brother." I took him by the hand, and I prayed for him. I said, "Lord, don't just give him a tent, but give him the chairs that go with it. And while You're doing that, Lord, give him a brand new organ. And while You're doing that, Lord, give him a new truck to carry it in."

The young man wasn't crying anymore. He was saying, "Yeah, Lord! May God answer the man of God's prayer!"

Six months later, that same young evangelist came and grabbed me and danced me around and said, "Thank you preacher! Thank you for taking that money!"

I said, "I'd like to have this on record — somebody thanking me for taking an offering."

He said, "God answered your prayer. God gave me a brand new tent with the chairs, the platform, the Hammond organ and a brand new truck, and it didn't cost me a dime. Thank God I obeyed His voice!"

When *you* trust God with an offering, you may not get the same return. But God knows just what you need. He responds to our faith and obedience. When we trust God even in our need, He knows how to open doors we never dreamed possible!

7

"But, Lord!"

Bishop Williams from Connecticut had invited me to conduct crusades; and during the offering, God told Brother Williams, "Give $100."

Brother Williams said, "Lord, I paid for the auditorium."

God said, "Give $200."

Brother Williams said, "But, Lord, I paid for the advertising."

God said, "Give $300."

Brother Williams said, "But, Lord, I —"

And God said, "Give $400."

Brother Williams said, "But, Lord —"

"Give $500."

Finally, Brother Williams said, "Yes, Lord!"

He was going to stop before God went any higher. He gave me that $500 gift, and I knew it was difficult for him, especially because he had sponsored the crusades, paid for the auditorium and so many details, and, besides, his congregation was trying to buy a new church.

That night Brother Williams said to me, "Brother Schambach, there's a church building I want. The Methodists who own it are moving out. Would you come down there and pray over that church for me?"

I said, "I'll walk around it. Sure will."

The next day the Methodist people gave that church to Brother Williams for one dollar bill. One dollar. He was thrilled.

The very next week, however, that church building burned to the ground. But Brother Williams' church still owned the property. Then God gave them the property next door too.

One night, I was surprised to see Brother Williams come dashing into a service in Arlington. He said, "Brother Schambach, that $500 God turned into $500,000."

His church now owned three blocks of property and two homes for their old folks, and they had just finished a brand new church building — all worth a half a million dollars. And it didn't cost him a dime. All it took was obedience to God!

8

Brother Thompson's Miracle

Brother Thompson was an old Baptist brother who came to my meeting in Brooklyn years ago. His arm was paralyzed; he couldn't use it. After prayer, God performed a miracle and healed that arm. Brother Thompson worked for Buick; he was a body man on automobiles. That's a very lucrative business in New York. Everybody gets their cars messed up. But Brother Thompson would rather have been working for himself.

I was receiving an offering after God healed Brother Thompson, and he told me, "You know, Brother Schambach, you scared the liver out of me when you asked us to give God the biggest thing we had. I'm a Baptist. We Baptists never give *anything* over a dollar."

I replied, "You Baptists don't have anything on the Pentecostal folks. Some of them come with change in their hands!"

I believe that many people give something when they go to church just to look like they're placing something in the plate — a little conscience money.

Brother Thompson had a twenty dollar bill in his wallet, and it was like pulling teeth to get it out of his billfold. But he turned it loose, and that twenty dollar bill was the start of a new life for Brother Thompson.

God began to bless him. A bit later he came to me and said, "Brother Schambach, I'm getting tired of working for somebody else. I want you to pray and ask God to put me in business for myself."

I laid hands on him and prayed, "Lord, let somebody work for *him*."

So he quit his job. When the Buick people found out he was going to open his own shop, they closed down their shop and sent him all their business! Now, instead of just getting a paycheck from someone else's business, he was making it all. Soon he had six men working for him.

And God kept blessing him. I'll never forget the day he called me on the phone. He said, "Brother Schambach, I believe you made a mistake."

I said, "What's that?"

He said, "You sent me a tax receipt for the year that says I gave $7,500. I think something's wrong."

I said, "Oh no, those books don't lie, brother."

He said, "Where did I get it all?"

I said, "That's the secret. The reason you got so much is because you gave so much."

9
"Old Red"

When I was in Bible school, my wife and I would go out into the hills of Missouri every Sunday morning and I would preach in a one-room schoolhouse. Farmers from all over that area would come. One little precious lady, eighty-three years of age, would walk three miles, take her stockings off, and wade through a creek just to come and hear me preach. Even *I* wouldn't do that to hear *me* preach! (I was still learning how!)

She invited us to her home for dinner. She told us to park the car when we got to the creek and walk the rest of the way. We took our shoes off and waded through the creek, just like she did every Sunday. But that Sunday morning I was preaching on a difficult doctrinal subject — tithing. I said, "Ten cents out of every dollar you ever get a hold of belongs to God."

There they sat, with smiles on their faces — which I knew was the wrong reaction. I wasn't getting the message through to them. So I said it again, and still they smiled. Finally it dawned on me, *You know why they're smiling: They don't have any money, and 10 percent of nothing is nothing! So I have to come at it from another way.*

It's amazing what comes out of you when you're anointed, I said, "If you have ten cows, one of those cows belongs to God." All the smiles left.

I knew they understood it now.

I said, "If you have 200 acres, 20 of them belong to God."

Nobody was smiling now.

After the service, a redheaded farmer came up to me, hands in his overall pockets. He said, "If my chickens lay 100 eggs every day, does God get 10 of the eggs?"

I said, "You got the message, brother. It's gratifying to know you got the message."

Without batting an eyelash, he looked me right in the eye and said, "You're not getting my eggs! Them chickens aren't laying anyway!"

I said, "You know why those chickens aren't laying? Because you're robbing God! Those chickens can't even live a normal life!"

I didn't know how right I was. Remember, I was just learning. He looked at me and said, "You mean to tell me if I give God what belongs to Him, those chickens will lay more eggs? Wait here!"

He got into that pickup truck and went back to the farm and brought a brown sack full of eggs. He laid them down at the altar. He came back to me, hands still in his overalls, and said, "You going to be here next Sunday?"

I said, "Yes, sir."

He said, "This better work!"

I was so young in the Lord, I didn't know whether it was going to work or not. I went back to the Bible that week. I didn't get much studying done. But I got a whole lot of praying done. I was praying, "Lord, bless those chickens! Lord, give them a double portion! Let them lay double yolks, Lord!"

The next Sunday, my wife and I headed out to that little town. I said, "Honey, do you see anybody standing in that schoolhouse?"

She said, "I believe somebody's there."

I said, "Does it have red hair?"

She said, "I'm not close enough to see that, yet."

Sure enough, it was Red waiting for me. But I couldn't see his face. I didn't know whether he was mad or glad. I brought my old DeSoto to a halt and pulled on the emergency brake. Old Red came running to the car. I don't ever like to be at a disadvantage, so I jumped out of the car. He grabbed hold of me and started dancing me around that DeSoto.

"Preach, man, it worked, brother!" he cried. "Praise God, it worked! It worked!"

I breathed easy for the first time all week. Then I looked around and said, "Hold it, Red, wait! Where's the tithe?" I believed I had a right to ask him for that. I said, "If we made the thing work, where's the tithe?"

Hands still in his overalls, he said, "In there, at the altar, Preach. Brought 'em early today."

I walked into that one-room schoolhouse, and sitting in front of that altar was a whole crate of eggs — twenty-five dozen. I looked at him and said, "What did you do, bring them *all*?"

His hands were still in his overalls. "Just the tithe, Preach. Just the tithe." From a brown sack to twenty-five dozen!

He threw his arms around me and said, "Preacher, I ain't going to rob God no more."

I looked at him and said, "Me neither."

I believe we've all had an apple out of that bag. Then we wonder why we're not blessed.

God rewards obedience.

10

That's My Cow in There

A twelve-year-old boy taught a whole crusade audience how to give.

Years ago in Seattle, two tornadoes tore through and destroyed our tent. The devil destroyed the tent; God didn't. But God can take a disaster and turn it around and work it for His glory. He's a master at that.

We could not continue services in the tent, so I looked for a building. The Civic Auditorium was available over the next seventeen days. We didn't miss a meeting. And before we left town, enough money came in to buy a brand new tent. The devil has no sense. The first tent was full of holes. God gave us a brand new one!

But a twelve-year-old boy started it off.

I received the offering one night, and I happened to see a little twelve-year-old walking down the aisle with a five-dollar bill in his hand. Tears were running down his face. You know how we human beings often make snap judgments and form first impressions. I thought, *I wonder what that kid is crying for? His mama gave him that five dollars. Maybe he didn't want to walk down here with it.*

He headed right for the bucket that I was holding. I said, "What are you crying for, boy?"

He threw the five dollars in the bucket. He said, "Brother Schambach, that's my cow in there!"

I said, "Your what?" I looked in the bucket. Here I was, wrong once again. His mama didn't send him with that five dollars, I knew I had a story there.

I put the bucket in one of the pastor's hands. I took the little boy aside and said, "Tell me about it."

"I always wanted a cow of my own," he said. "But we lived in the city limits, and there's an ordinance that says you can't have a cow in the backyard. But nine months ago, Dad moved out into the country. And he called me and said I could have a cow now — but I had to pay for it. For nine months I've been saving my dimes. I've been running errands. I picked up a paper route. I get up at four in the morning and deliver newspapers. I've been saving five dollars for nine months!"

I said, "Why are you putting that cow money in?"

He said, "I heard God's voice."

My God, that's the miracle to me! Giving five dollars is no miracle. But can you imagine getting a twelve-year-old boy to hear the voice of God? I asked, "How did you know it was God?"

He said, "He called me by my name. He said if I gave the cow money, He would give me the cow."

I looked at him and said, "Are you sure God told you that?"

"Yes, sir, He told me that."

I said, "Then dry up those tears! You're getting the best end of the deal!"

While the other folks were bringing their offerings, I sort of held on to his shoulder. I told all those people in that Civic Auditorium what I just told you about that boy.

Then a big 6'7", 270-pound usher in bib overalls got up. He started crying. He walked up, and I said, "What are you crying for, brother?"

He said, "God just spoke to me."

I said, "What did God tell you?"

He said, "He told me to give that boy a cow."

I looked up and down at him. I learned this lesson a long time ago: The folks with the fancy suits don't have the money. It's the guys wearing the overalls. (The guys with the suits on have all their money in the suits!) So I kind of did a double take on him and said, "Brother, do you have a cow?" (I wanted to make sure that boy got his cow.)

"I got thousands of them, Brother Schambach," he replied. He was the biggest rancher in the state of Washington.

The following Saturday he had a Polaroid picture shot of the boy with his cow.

The rancher said, "Brother Schambach, I wish you could have been out at the ranch today. That boy came out with his daddy in a rented trailer to pick up his cow. I told him to go pick out any one he wanted. You know, that rascal picked the best one I had! And he never even thanked me for it. He just put his arm around that cow and raised the other arm up and said, 'Thank you, Jesus, for my cow!'"

That's what he *should* have done, because the cattle on a thousand hills belong to God! (Ps. 50:10.) And He knows how to speak to somebody to turn one of them loose.

After that little boy told his story, you should have seen how much money came in that offering. You don't have to beg people to give. You show them how God blesses, and they'll want to get in on that blessing. Luke 6:38 says, "Give, and it shall be given unto you." So you have to plant the seed first. Notice the word "give" — and then it shall be given unto you. God was teaching that boy a principle, and teaching me a principle through that boy.

11
Giving in Haiti

This Bible I preach has to work in Haiti — or India or Mozambique or Japan — just like it works here. If it doesn't work everywhere, then it's not the Bible.

Haiti is one of the poorest nations in our hemisphere. The first time I flew to Haiti, I was met by a group of preachers. Instead of greeting me with "Welcome to Haiti," they looked at me and said, "You're not taking an offering here!"

I said, "When is the next plane out of here? You men didn't call for me. The Holy Ghost sent me down here. I'm going to take an offering, because the Bible instructs us to teach our people to give."

"But our people have no money! We're pastors. We don't even receive an offering."

I said, "Then I hold you gentlemen responsible for the poverty of your nation. If I can't make this Bible work in Haiti, I'll burn the thing. Either it's the truth or it's a lie; either it's God's book or it's man's book. I believe it's God's book."

I began to preach to the people and receive an offering from them. Those poor people opened their hearts in a wonderful way and gave about $15,000. At that time, that was unheard of in the history of Haiti. I told those pastors, "Your people need to learn the Gospel here in Haiti like people know it in Atlanta and New York City! If people can make it work there, they can make it work here!"

I'm reminded of Mother Valez up in Brooklyn. She's a black sister there who taught me a lesson in how to give. I told this story to the Haitian pastors. Haiti is a black nation, and here was a white dude asking them to give some money! I stood up in front of all of them and said, "A black lady in Brooklyn taught me how to give."

Mother Valez, one of the oldest people in my church, came to me one night, tears coming down her face. She said, "Brother Schambach, God told me to give you my rent money."

I said, "What? When is your rent due?"

She said, "In three days."

I folded it back in her hand. I said, "Go pay your rent, woman! What's wrong with you?"

She said, "You don't understand. You didn't ask for this, God did! Are you trying to cheat me out of my blessing? Now take it!"

I took it. The next night, Mother Valez came again and put a $100 bill in my hand. "See what you almost cheated me out of?" she said.

She knew something I didn't know. She and I had been praying for her sons to be saved. She said, "Brother Schambach, those two boys you and I have been praying and fasting for got saved this morning! Not only that, God blessed me with $1,000! Here's the tithe off of it! My God, I'm blessed!"

I told that story in Haiti. The next night a little Haitian woman came to me with $100. Seventy thousand people were there for that service, and I wanted all of them to hear what this little lady had to say.

She said, "Remember that story Pastor told last night about that woman in Brooklyn? If God can do it in Brooklyn, He can do it here in Haiti. My rent is $160, and it's due tomorrow. I only have $100. So I'm just going to give it to God. They won't take it anyway. I'm going to trust God to do it!"

I thought, *Oh, Lord.*

And all the Haitian preachers on that platform were sitting there saying, "Oh, Lord. This ain't New York. This is Port-au-Prince."

All of a sudden, I saw a man coming from the middle of that crowd. He said, "God spoke to me. He told me to pay that woman's rent for three months. Here's the check for it."

If God can make it work in Atlanta, God can make it work in Haiti! God can make it work over in Sudan! I don't care where it is, God's Word is real — and it works!

12

Giving to God, Not to Man

I preached in Buffalo, New York, in forty-six inches of snow. I had 1,500 people out in an auditorium. That's a lot of folks in forty-six inches of snow. I told the folks I was going to receive an offering. A lady stood up and yelled, "Brother Schambach, an evangelist came to town, and I gave him $1,500, and I didn't get anything back."

I thought, *Oh, Lord, she is going to kill my offering. Will You hush that woman up?*

Then she said, "A second evangelist came to town, and I gave him $2,500. And I still didn't get anything back. Then a third evangelist came to town, and I gave him $3,000. I still didn't get anything back." Then she sat down.

I said, "Sister, stand back up. How much do you have left?"

She said, "Nothing!"

I said, "For the past minute and a half, we have heard you talk. Three times you said, 'I gave to an evangelist,' and not once did you say, 'I gave to God.' There's your answer."

When you give, you're not giving to the church. I hear folks say, "I give to the church." No wonder they're messed up. "I give to my church." "I give to the preacher." No, you don't. When you give, you are giving to God. I want you to see this because if I can turn you around so you put your giving in its proper perspective then you will be blessed.

People say to me, "I pay my tithes." No, you don't. How can you pay something that doesn't even belong to you? The tithe is the Lord's. That belongs to God. If you make $200 a week, you don't make $200; you make $180. That $20 right off the top belongs to God.

I believe that the tithe belongs to God. That tithe should be given where you are being fed, right there in your local church. And I preach that. I'm an evangelist, and I want your *offering*.

God said,

> Will a man rob God? Yet ye have robbed me. But ye say, Wherein have we robbed thee? In tithes and offerings.
>
> Bring ye all the tithes into the storehouse, that there may be meat in mine house, and prove me now herewith, saith the Lord of hosts, if I will not open you the windows of heaven, and pour you out a blessing, that there shall not be room enough to receive it.
>
> Malachi 3:8,10

13
God Provides Food

My mama was a woman of faith. Mama had twelve children, and six of us were at home. When you're trusting God for six kids, it takes some faith. Pop was laid off from the railroad. When it was time for supper, Mom never asked you what you wanted. We never asked what it was; we were just glad to get it. We all had our same spot around the table. One time she called us out for supper. My place was next to the oven. Jim sat next to me; Leroy on the other side — he was bigger. I felt that oven, and it was cold. I nudged Jim. I looked down at the dishes, and they were empty. But Mom had called us here to eat.

My mother was a woman of God! She sat us kids around that table, and she said, "All right, now, quiet. We are going to pray and thank God for the food."

I nudged Jim again. I said, "Mom flipped her wig. 'Thank God for the food.' There isn't any food."

She was oblivious to natural surroundings. Anybody can thank God for a hot dog in his hand. You can thank God for food in your refrigerator. But she was thanking God for nothing. She started to pray. "Lord, in Jesus' name, bless all the missionaries who don't have anything."

I nudged Jim again. "We're missionaries. We don't have anything."

But Mama went right on. "Lord, we thank You for what You have provided."

My one eye came open. I thought that mashed potato dish was going to fill up right on the spot. I thought that meat plate was going to have meat on it. Still nothing was there. Mom was still thanking God for it. She said, "Lord, You have never failed me. The Lord will provide. I thank You for taking care of my family."

Inside I was saying, *I wish she would hurry up. I know somebody who has some food. I'll go up there and get some as soon as she gets done.* As soon as she said, "Amen," our back door opened. In popped Sister Landis with two chickens already stuffed and cooked. Then in came a man with a jug of milk and two loaves of homemade bread.

I nudged Jim again. "Hey! Mom got it, boy! Mom knows what she's talking about!"

I'm talking about a prevailing kind of faith that holds on to the horns of the altar. (1 Kings 1:50,51.) Don't give up! Thank God for it. The answer is on the way. Get your eyes off that situation. Get your eyes off that trouble in your family relationship. Get your eyes off the balance in your checkbook. Get your eyes *on* the promise. If God said it, He will do it. He will not have His seed begging bread. You are a child of God. He will make a way where there is no way. Hang on to the horns of the altar until that answer gets here.

14
Multiplying Money

I had a tent up over in East St. Louis some years ago. I'll never forget a little woman — she must have been sixty-eight years of age — who came to me. (I believe she must have gone to be with the Lord by now.) She said to me, "Brother Schambach, I want you to pray that God will let me rent a bus."

I thought, *What in the world would she want a bus for? That's the craziest request I have ever heard.* So I asked her why she wanted a bus. She said, "I want to take a crowd of people to hear Kathryn Kuhlman."

I said, "You want me to pray and ask God to give you money to get a bus so you can take a crowd of people out of my tent meeting to go hear a woman preach?" But I prayed. I asked God to bless her with it.

She said, "I already have $400, but I need a little over $800."

I took the paper sack of money she had, and I prayed. On Monday night she came back shouting. I never saw a woman that old shout like she did. She said, "Brother Schambach, I went home and counted that money; there was $500. I called my husband out to count it; I thought I made a mistake. He sat down and counted it, and he got $600. I put it back into the bag, took it down to the bank the next morning and had the bankers count it. They counted $700." The teller asked if she wanted to deposit it, but she didn't. She had the money put back into the bag. She took that bag down to the Greyhound Bus rental and said, "Here's my money for the bus." When they counted, there was a little over $800 — enough to get her bus. She took a busload of people to hear Kathryn Kuhlman preach.

The Lord will provide! He will satisfy the hunger pains of the people. He rented a bus for a woman. I don't care what your need is; Jesus is a miracle-working God, and He will perform a miracle in your life!

What is your need? You know, people get into a rut many times, and they consider miracles only in the aspect of healing. But God is a miracle-working God in *every phase of life*!

15
My Mom, the Bank

I believe it must have been my mama who first taught me how to give. Back in those days, Mama was our bank. We had six kids at home. Mama had a little purse in her pocketbook with all of our names on it. I'll never forget the first paper route I got. I was making a dollar and a half a week. I brought it home to Mama. I said, "Put that in your pocketbook."

She said, "A dollar and a half — God's given you the ability to earn that this week. Fifteen cents of that belongs to God."

I said, "Give Him a quarter, Mom." I felt like I was in high finance. "Give Him a quarter."

She said, "Well, that's scriptural. That's giving God the tithe plus an offering."

Before very long, that total started to move up. I was making three and a half dollars a week. She said, "Now remember, thirty-five cents of that belongs to God."

I said, "Give Him half a dollar."

Then, as a young lad, I worked around a farmers' market. Farmers used to come in there, and I used to help sell their stuff. I saw a florist there; she was buying little crockery pots to put flowers in. I had seen people throwing those pots away — the very item she was paying money to acquire. She agreed to pay me a nickel a piece for every pot I could bring her. I got my little old wagon and went out in every backyard I could find. I stacked that little red wagon up with pots and took them to the market and got twenty dollars. That's more than my dad made. I brought that twenty dollars home to Mom.

She said, "Son, two dollars belong to God."

I said, "Give Him five." I felt good about this. "Give Him five, Mama."

In high school, during World War II, I started working in a machine shop: L.B. Smith. I'll never forget working on that grinder. My job was to grind the bushings down. I was making $150 a week, going to high school. I'll never forget bringing that first check home to Mom. The job paid every two weeks.

She said, "Remember now, Son, thirty dollars of that belongs to God."

I said, "Hold it, Mom. Whoa! Back up here, now. What's that preacher going to do with my money?" You see, when you're making two dollars, you don't mind giving God twenty cents. But the more God blesses you, the more you can tithe, and it starts adding up.

My mama said, "Son, you aren't giving that to the preacher. You're giving that to God."

I said, "I'm not going to do it!"

She said, "Then suffer!"

Mom was smart. I think she was a psychiatrist. She never did study for it, but, boy, was she bright.

I said, "I saw a nice pair of shoes down there at Flagg Brothers. I'm going to get them."

She said, "You're going to suffer."

Before the week was over, I was back. "Mom will you lend me some money? C'mon, Mom. You have money. I'll give it to you on payday."

She said, "You're never going to have a payday if you keep robbing God." She was a psychiatrist! She just laid it on me.

I got in a hole so bad I couldn't get out. I came back to her and said, "Mom, how can I get out of this?" She said, "Pay your tithes. You don't start over again. You've got to go back and pay those back tithes."

I said, "If I do that, I won't have any spending money for four weeks."

She said, "Then do it. I'm telling you how you're going to get blessed."

I appreciate the wisdom and the knowledge that my mother fed into me when I was just a young lad. The blessing of God comes when you give God what belongs to Him. God said, "You rob me with the tithe and the offering." (Mal. 3:8.)

Someone has asked, "How much of an offering do I have to give?" Whatever He puts his finger on — that's what He expects us to be obedient to. The bottom line is obedience. That is what God rewards. He doesn't reward you on the amount of your offering; He's looking for your obedience, as a child of God, to His command.

16
New Car Deal

A man, who used to work with me, saved his money to buy a beautiful 1963 Pontiac. Oh, it was a pretty car. It was used, but he polished it up. He must have paid $650 for that car, and that was big money when he bought it. He was proud of that Pontiac. He kept it shining. You could comb your hair just by looking at your reflection in the paint. And after he got it all polished, God said to him, "Give that car away to that man who just walked under the tent."

My friend said, "What? I don't know that man!"

God said, "I do. Give him the car."

He had been working on it all day long to get a perfect shine on it, and now God was saying to give it to a stranger who had just walked under the tent! My friend could have withheld; but he was so tender in his spirit, he walked back and gave the man the keys. He said, "Here, God told me to give you the keys to my automobile, and here's the title to it."

This old boy was just thrilled! He said, "Wonderful! I've been praying for three days for a car!"

My man's face fell, and he said, "Three days? Shoot, I was praying for a car for a year before I finally got it. And I didn't have it two days before God said to give it to you. And you've only been praying three days." But he did what God told him.

The next night somebody came and handed him the keys to a brand new Pontiac and said, "God told me to give you this."

God gave him a brand new car in place of the used one he gave away! You don't need a used car; you need a brand new one. When you take your hands off of something and commit it into the hands of God, being obedient to His voice, nothing but blessing can follow you all the days of your life.

17
Building in Newark

I'll never forget the first church building I bought. It was an old Jewish YWHA in New Jersey. I rented it for three months, preached in it, and so many folks got saved in it, I thought I might as well just buy the building and establish a church. But there was no way — I didn't even have a bank account.

One day while we were still renting, I was studying my message. I was going to preach on Deuteronomy 11:24 that says **Every place whereon the soles of your feet shall tread shall be yours....** Oh, Lord! I knew I wasn't just preaching to those people, I was preaching to me! I laid hands on about 500 people that night, but I couldn't wait to close that service.

After the service, I got my Bible, went out, and I said to some of my preacher friends, "Come with me. We're going to walk around the building and lay some footprints down. I'm going to claim this thing."

I couldn't buy it. I had never had a bank account. I had never written a check. I didn't have any sense, but I had faith.

When I told my preacher friends that I was going to walk around that building and claim it, they said, "We'll wait in the car. You go ahead and walk."

I've learned this: When you put your faith to work, you've got to do it all by yourself. God said that every bit of ground that the soles of *your* feet tread on, you shall possess it.

I walked around that building. And the next day they put a "For Sale" sign on the lawn. I pulled it out and took it down to the realtor. I said, "Who put this on my property?" He thought I was crazy.

He said, "What do you want to offer me for that building?"

I said, "Nothing."

"Well," he said, "Come back when you have money."

I said, "Now hold on here a minute. I believe in starting low."

He said, "We just had an offer of $265,000. An insurance company owns it, and I know they won't sell it for less than that."

Just then the Holy Ghost said, "Offer them $75,000." Now, if He had told me to offer a million, I would have done it, because I didn't have a dime anyway. There's no difference between $75,000 and a million if you don't have anything at all. Zero is zero. That's why it's always good to obey God. You don't have to be afraid of anything. You started with nothing, you're going to end with nothing.

I said, "I'll give you $75,000."

He picked up the phone and called the chairman of the board of this insurance company. He turned away from me, but I could hear him saying, "I have a crazy preacher in my office. I told him you folks turned down an offer of $265,000, but he told me to offer you $75,000. I told him there's no way you'll do it. And...what did you say? Would you say that one more time? Well, all right. It's your building. Yes, sir."

He hung up the phone and turned around to me. "He told me to sell it to you for $75,000."

I said, "What happened?"

He said, "They were just meeting there. They had such a great year in life insurance that they said to give it to the preacher for $75,000, and they would take a loss on the taxes. You're not so dumb are you, preacher?"

I said, "No, sir."

He said, "Now, how much money do you have for a down payment?"

I said, "Nothing."

He asked for $35,000 down. God provided $25,000. The night before I had to come up with the money, we were still $10,000 short, and I didn't know what we'd do. I went home and went to bed. A local preacher asked me, "What are you going to do?"

I said, "Nothing. I didn't do anything when I first started; I'm not going to do anything now. There's no time to worry now. There's no way God's going to let the devil whip Him in a business deal. God's the best businessman I've ever seen. He always finishes what He starts."

I sat in that office the next day and waited until ten minutes until noon. Noon was the deadline. A little woman came walking up. I ran out to her and said, "Give it to me! Give me it!"

She said, "How do you know I have something for you?"

I said, "I'll talk to you later; just turn it loose and give it to me. It's got to be you. God's never cut it so close!" She reached into her purse and took out a $10,000 cashier's check. I grabbed that thing and went down to the bank. The building belonged to me!

After it was over, one of those preachers who wouldn't march around the building with me in the first place called me on the phone from Englewood and said, "I found a building here in Englewood that I want for a church. Come on over and walk around it for me."

I said, "Well, I'm about twenty-eight minutes from you, but I'll make it in twenty. Wait for me. But remember, brother, if I use my feet, it's going to be my building!" He never even bothered to hang up — just left the phone dangling and ran over to that building. But he didn't just march around it, he raced around it and laid down his size ten tracks. Guess what? God gave him his building!"

God has an inheritance for you that's different from somebody else's! Learn how to trust Him, and He'll bring you through.

But you know, I've got one regret. I wish I would have walked around the whole block. It works! It works! You can trust Him! Anybody can trust Him when the checkbook's filled. But it takes faith to trust

Him when the balance says double zero! You've got to step out on the water! And God will make a way where there is no way!

18
Obedience Pays Off

There was a man who had a truck, but he needed a different truck. He was driving an old piece of junk, really. Did you ever drive one of those things? You've got to lay hands on it before it starts? Then you have to lay hands on it to make it stop!

This man gave an offering, and the Lord saw his heart. Often when you're in financial need, you think maybe God is going to talk to somebody wealthy to come and give you help. But don't even wonder how He is going to do it, because God's just going to turn around and do it some other way. This man came back with one of the craziest stories I have ever heard in my life.

He was driving that old wreck of a truck down the streets of Brooklyn, and God spoke to him and said, "Stop the truck! Get out of the truck and lift up the hood." So he did. Then God said, "Look down by the carburetor." Now God would know better than to tell R. W. Schambach to look by the carburetor, because I'm not mechanical, and I'd be just as likely to open the trunk. But this man knew where the carburetor was. God talks to you on your level.

So the man looked down under the carburetor. He said, "Am I losing my mind? I'm looking, but I don't see anything but a carburetor." So he shut the hood and got back in and started driving down the street again.

But God said, "I told you to stop this truck and look down there by that carburetor."

So he stopped the truck and lifted the hood. He said, "Lord, I'm looking."

God said, "Look with your hand!"

Sometimes you can't see with your eyes — especially where the carburetor is. You've got to look with your hand. When he put his hand down by the carburetor, he got a hold of something that didn't belong there. It was a roll all covered with grease. He pulled it out — a whole wad of $100 bills wrapped up in grease. Whoever owned that truck before probably had tried to hide his money there. It was such a good hiding place that when he died, nobody found it. God arranged for my friend to buy that wreck. Soon he had traded that thing in and bought a brand new truck. God has a way of working things out! You're not on your own. He doesn't turn you loose just to do your own thing. He is leading you! There's **a pillar of a cloud** by day and there's **a pillar of fire** by night! (Ex. 13:21.) I'm talking about the Holy Ghost Who will lead you and guide you and direct you. He will make a way! He has a strategy in mind for you!

19
Power Partner Pennaman

Our ministry has what we call Power Partners. Power Partners not only pray with me, but they help the ministry financially every month. They give $25 a month, and God blesses them.

I met a black brother in New York, Brother Pennaman. I went to preach at Madision Square Garden, and he sent me a letter. I opened that letter and a $100 check fell out. I opened it again, and a $500 check dropped out. After that I shook it, but that was the end of it, except for one of the most beautiful letters I had ever read. It blessed me.

He told me, "Brother Schambach, ever since you started Power Partners, I wanted to give, but I've been on welfare. You know, when you're on welfare, you just don't have enough money for everything. But I sent you twenty-five cents a week. That's a dollar a month. God started to bless me. Before long, I could send you five dollars a month. You were praying for me, and the folks down there at your office were praying. Then I started sending ten dollars a month, and finally I became a Power Partner. You sent me that pin and my Bible. Then God got me off welfare."

That's what I desire. I want to get folks off the welfare system. I want God to bless His people. Now you read this story. It will bless your soul. This man said, "Brother Schambach, I started getting blessed. The city gave me a job managing some apartment buildings. I was making so much money that I changed from twenty-five dollars a month. The blessing of God kept being poured out on me. I had more money than I knew what to do with, so I made it fifty dollars a month."

I mean, he was blessing me now!

He said, "Brother Schambach, now I've got two apartment buildings that I'm managing for the city. I'm sending you $100 a month now. I never made so much money in all my life. This $100 check is my Power Partner pledge for the month. That $500 check — I just got so much I don't know what to do with it. Just put it anywhere you want to."

That's a man who came from the welfare system, who couldn't afford to give twenty-five cents a week!

When you give to God first, and you make a commitment, then God is going to see that you get blessed. When you're paying your tithes, don't give God what's left. A lot of times we take the rent out. Then we pay the phone bill, then the light bill. And we say, "Lord, this is what I have left now. I'm going to give You some."

That's all wrong. No wonder you're messed up. You take God's right off the top. Say, "Lord, this belongs to You. You're first in my life." When you start giving God what belongs to Him, you're headed for the greatest blessing of your life.

20
Pray Specifically

A young man in my church came to me and told me he wanted a job. When I asked him what kind of job, he said he would take anything. So I laid my hand on him and prayed that God would give him a job shining shoes! He ducked out from under may hand and said, "I don't want to shine shoes!'

So I asked him again what kind of job he wanted, and he said he wanted to get the computer job he had applied for. I said, "Now you're asking for something." I laid my hands on him and prayed, "Lord, he already applied for that computer job. Give it to him in the name of Jesus." When I finished praying I said, "Get dressed in the morning. Set the alarm for 6 a.m. Get up and be waiting down there. It's your job, mister."

I didn't see him for a month, but when I did, he had a paycheck from that job! It was a $500 check, and he was excited, because that was just one week's wages. I said, "That sure beats shining shoes, doesn't it?" and I put that check back in his hands.

He said, "Oh, no. I'm giving God the first fruit. He's getting it all. You taught me something, preacher. You have not because you ask not. You receive not because you ask amiss." (James 4:2,3.)

I want you to know you can have what you want! Come to the Source! It belongs to you! In the name of Jesus, **Ask, and it shall be given you; seek, and ye shall find; knock, and it shall be opened unto you** (Matt.7:7). You are the recipient of that miracle. It belongs to you. Don't be denied!

21
My $100 Pledge

I was fresh out of Bible college, and my wife and I were pastoring a church in Western Pennsylvania. They had just moved us into a brand new parsonage with all brand new furniture. When we moved there she thought, *This is it. I'm going to stay until Jesus comes.*

This was back in the middle 50's, so the salary that the church paid their pastor was $50 a week. I thought I was in hog heaven. I didn't have a bank account, but I was happy. I was in the will of God.

I was invited to speak in my hometown at a meeting with several important evangelists. I wondered how I was going to get time off to go to that meeting. I knew if I could get there, I wouldn't have to stay at a motel, because Mom lived there, and I'd stay at home. I didn't have to go to a restaurant — not when Mom's around. She provides the best cooking in the world!

Well, the church gave me time off to go down there, and I sat on that platform every night with all those sponsoring pastors — even though I was pastoring in the Pittsburgh area, 200 miles away from there. On the last Sunday afternoon of that meeting, Oral Roberts introduced something new.

He stood before those people under that tent and he said, "God told me to go on television."

My first reaction was, Oh, won't that be wonderful? Put Jack Benny out of business. Put the revival on from a tent!

He said, "God promised me 1,000 people will give $100 to pay for the production cost of that television program."

That doesn't seem like much money today, but that was a whole lot of money then. One hundred thousand dollars. I was sitting up there on that platform; I bowed my head and I said, "Yes, Lord, speak to the people!" As if I'm not people, you know. That's the way we often pray, isn't it?

God spoke to my heart right away and said, "Son, I want you to be one of them."

I shouted a little louder, "Lord, talk to the people who have it! Yes, Lord!" — trying to drown out His voice now. We're all made out of the same stuff. I was trying to push it over on somebody else now. I said, "Lord, you know I have nothing. I'm going to have to borrow twenty dollars from my brother to get back home."

That was my faith. And guess what? I *did* end up borrowing twenty dollars from my brother — because I had confessed it.

But God spoke to me again. He said, "Son, I'm not going to ask you anymore. This will be the last time. I know you don't have it. But I'll give it to you."

I said, "Oh, that's different." I leaped out of my seat, and I jumped down there with the rest of the 1,300 people who had come forward. Some 1,300 came forward because God has a way of giving more than what you ask for.

Brother Roberts prayed, "Lord, many of these folks don't have the money, but I'm asking You to give it back ten times over."

That got my attention. My computer brain already had the figures itemized out. I said, "Yes, Lord! Answer the prayer of that man of God!" I went back home, and I didn't have the money to pay my pledge. But God called me not long after that, to go on the evangelistic field. I told my wife, "Don't get settled in, honey. We've got to be on the move. We're going to be traveling."

God knew that I needed a trailer house for my family, and I didn't have any money. So when I resigned the pastorate, the church took an offering for me that Sunday morning. Up to that point, I had never seen that much money in all my life. To the dollar, to the penny, it was $1,000.

My mind went back to that tent. The man of God prayed that my $100 pledge would be multiplied. I hadn't given it yet, but here God multiplied it and put it in my hand. I learned another principle of giving under that tent. First thing I did was pay the tithe off of it: I sent that $100 pledge.

That left me with $900, and God led me to a Christian man who sold trailer homes in Reading, Pennsylvania. When he found out I was an evangelist and I was going to use the trailer to go on the road, he said, "Preacher, the first thing I'm going to do is knock $1,000 off the cost of this trailer."

Brother Roberts prayed and asked God to multiply it tenfold, but God gave it back twenty times. Exceeding, abundantly, above what you can ask or even think. You can always give what you have in your hand, but it takes faith to give something you do not have. And I learned that lesson way back in 1954.

22
My Used Truck Lot

Brother Clendennen was with me in Tampa, Florida, some years ago. We had the tent up there. We used to have gasoline rigs, and we had to fast and pray to get those trucks to the next location.

That bothered me! Here I was, a man of God, taking a tent around the country, pulling all these trucks, chugging down the highway, and here would come old Budweiser and Schlitz trucks and blow us off the road. We had a big placard plastered on the side of our truck that said, "Signs, Wonders and Miracles." It looked like the whole miracle was that our truck was moving at all! Meanwhile, the devil had the finest equipment money could buy. I used to say a lot of our equipment came over on the Mayflower — that's how old it was.

Finally, I started catching some faith in order to update the equipment. We found some good equipment right there in Tampa. A guy who sold some Kenworth trailers — the Cadillac of the rigs — told me my credit was good, and he would get me six Kenworth rigs that we could pay off on installments.

One night that tent was jammed; I had about 3,000 people in there. And God spoke to me. I had about twenty preachers on the platform. God said to me, "Son, give one of those trucks to that particular preacher on the platform."

It wasn't like He was asking me to give a twenty dollar bill; He was asking me to give a truck worth thousands of dollars. So I hit that platform, and I grabbed the microphone. You know, sometimes the best way to give is to get up in front of 3,000 people and tell it, because then your word is out and you've *got* to follow through. That's one way to give the devil a black eye.

So I got up in front of all those folks and said, "God told me to give one of our trucks to that preacher." And I pointed him out.

The power of God suddenly hit him, and he leaped off of that platform and ran around that tent shouting. Then he came back and got me and he said, "Dance with me!"

I said, "You dance! You're getting the truck. I'm not dancing."

I didn't feel like dancing. Sometimes God tells you to do something, and you don't understand why, and you don't feel very good about it. That's how this was.

Our headquarters, at that time, were in Ellwood City, Pennsylvania. And this was Friday. On Monday morning, I knew my secretary would be at the office so I called her and told her to send the paperwork on the truck to that preacher. She said, "Did you sell him that truck?"

I said, "No, ma'am. I didn't sell it. I gave it to him."

She said, "For nothing?" Well, that's generally what you do when you give something. You just give it. She said, "What did you do that for?" She kept all the books, you know. She banked all the money. She paid all the bills.

I said, "I did it because God said so!"

She said, "Well that's different."

And that *is* different, isn't it? You don't do something just because a preacher tells you to; but when God tells you to do something, then you better do it. That's the bottom line. I learned that a long time ago. When God tells you, He's doing it for your good.

But my secretary went on to say, "Brother Schambach, will you sit down wherever you are? There's a man in your office right now. He's a truck driver."

I said, "I don't need any truck drivers. In fact, I just got rid of a truck. I have an *extra* truck driver."

She said, "He doesn't want a job! This man, who's sitting in your office, is a long-distance trucker from Pittsburgh to Frisco. All he does is haul from Pittsburgh to San Francisco. Then he picks up another load and brings it back to Pittsburgh. He listens to you on the Wheeling station, Iowa, and Frisco, and superpower stations. He says he gets you going and coming. Now he says God has called him to preach, so he's going to Bible college. Coming back through Iowa he was listening to you late at night when the Holy Ghost talked to him and told him to drive his Kenworth diesel to Ellwood City, Pennsylvania and give it to Brother Schambach."

I said, "Give it to me? Make him sign the papers, quick!"

That was our first Kenworth. Today we have six Kenworths. They are all paid for, and they belong to God.

23
Tithing Opens Blind Eyes

A little woman came to our crusades four days in a row. She was blind in one eye, and she didn't get healed. I'll never forget when A. A. Allen said to her, "You're not doing something God asked you to do."

She said, "I know that."

"Well, why are you wanting me to pray for you? Get on out of here and do what God told you to do."

She came back the second night, still blind in that eye. "Did you do what God told you to do?"

"No!"

"Go right on. I'm not wasting my prayers."

Third night, same thing.

Fourth night, she came again. The man of God said, "Did you do what God told you to do?"

"No!" She was trying to sneak by him in the healing line. She turned around, got halfway down that ramp, and she stopped. She said, "All right, Lord! I'll pay my tithes!" When she said that, the blind eye was opened. Nobody had to lay hands on her.

Disobedience is sin. And there are hindrances to the blessings of God. That woman found it out the hard way. Am I telling you if you don't pay your tithes that you're disobeying God? Yes! That's in the Book. Just like **I am the Lord that healeth thee** (Ex. 15:26) is in the Book. You can't cut it up and just believe what you want to. You've got to believe everything in the Book and be obedient to God. How can you rob God? By not paying your tithes and offerings. He said, "Prove me and see if I will not open the windows of heaven upon you!"

24

Giving in Trinidad

When it comes time to give, it's a blessing.

I conducted crusades in Trinidad, down in the Caribbean, among the poor folks down there. I followed Dan Betzer, the radio speaker for the Assemblies of God organization. He was there a week before me. I came in to close it out. I was there for three nights. The missionary who put this event on said, "Brother Schambach, the budget for this entire revival is $38,000." I think he was trying to tell me something, but I didn't care what the budget was. I was a guest. He asked me to come down there to preach.

So I said, "Well, you've been going on here about three weeks. You probably have it already met. How much has come in so far?"

He said, "Four thousand dollars."

I said, "You had better let me take the offering tonight."

Trinidad is 50 percent black and 50 percent Indian. There are a lot of Indians from India; they have immigrated there. It was a mixed audience that night. God started performing miracles. Blind eyes began to open. Demons were cast out. When God begins to manifest His power, the first thing people want to do is give God something. I prayed and asked God to touch the hearts of the people to give. That night, when I received the offering, $70,000 came in.

The missionary cried all night long. He couldn't sleep. The next night we went back. I said, "We don't have to receive offerings now; the meeting is paid for."

But people came and said, "I didn't have it last night. I want to give tonight." And it was more than the previous night. In three nights' time, $210,000 — in Trinidad! Of course, we left it all there for the churches. I didn't even spend a dime of it. One gentleman brought me five $100 bills and said, "I just want you to take these home as a souvenir."

I said, "Nothing doing. That's going in the offering. I'm not taking anything out of here. We came to give it to God."

Now I told this same story to a Full Gospel Businessmen's meeting. I said, "If I can raise an offering of $70,000 down in Trinidad, I had better do more than that tonight." In five minutes, $200,000 came in — enough to pay every bill they had. God is a miraculous God!

25
Beer Business Tithes?

There was a pastor who invited me to come to Philadelphia to preach and to help him raise some money to buy a church building. Do you know why I went? Because he told me a story. I love the man for this.

He needed $20,000 for a down payment for a building. Somehow a businessman in the Philadelphia area found out he needed it, and he went out to see that preacher. The preacher was having a counseling session with one of the little ladies in his church. The man stormed right into his office unannounced and said, "I don't wait for any preacher."

The pastor said, "You'll have to excuse me. I'm counseling a lady from my church."

The man said, "How dare you treat me like this! I heard you needed money! I've got a $20,000 check in my pocket that I brought over here for you. I have preachers in my office waiting to see me, begging for money every day."

The pastor said, "You've never seen me in your office, have you, mister? I don't care what you've got in your pocket. You go outside and wait until I get done with this little lady."

But then the man told this pastor his name, and the pastor recognized it. He said, "Are you the man who manufactures the beer with your name on the bottles?"

The man said, "I'm that man."

The pastor looked him right in the eye and said, "You keep your $20,000. Maybe you think you can appease God with an offering and ease your conscience, but I've got babies in my Sunday school going without milk because their daddies are drinking the booze you're making. You think you can give God a $20,000 check and make that right? I wouldn't touch your money with a 10-foot pole."

When I heard that story, I told the pastor, yes, I'll come to your church and help you raise that money. I went to his church and preached. God brought in $20,000 — not from millionaires, but from the little widow women. God doesn't need the devil's money. God wants to bless His own people.

The church is bought and paid for today. It was paid for by the people of the church who didn't have much money. God blessed them in order to bring it in!

26
Fertile Ground

Now that you've read these exciting testimonies of Christians just like you and me, whose prayers were answered when they were obedient to God, I know that you must be inspired and anxious to keep obeying God and receiving the desires of your heart! What happened for these brothers and sisters can happen for you!

But did you ever stop to think...God has given you seed to sow, and He expects you to drop that seed on fertile ground. Remember the parable of the sower in Luke 8:5-8?

> A sower went out to sow his seed: and as he sowed, some fell by the way side; and it was trodden down, and the fowls of the air devoured it.
>
> And some fell upon a rock; and as soon as it was sprung up, it withered away, because it lacked moisture.
>
> And some fell among thorns; and the thorns sprang up with it, and choked it.
>
> And other fell on good ground, and sprang up, and bare fruit an hundredfold.

The way I see it, that man wasted three-quarters of the seed he had to work with. The first three places where he tried sowing were very unproductive: in one place, birds carried the seed away; in another place, the seedlings died without water; in another place thorns sprang up and choked out the crop. But in the last place, in the good, fertile ground, every seed multiplied itself a hundredfold! If you had your choice and you were the sower, would you want to sow 75 percent of your seed in bad ground and just lose it, or would you want to sow 100 percent in good ground and reap that hundredfold harvest?

I hope that after reading all these wonderful testimonies of people who sowed in faith and reaped a wonderful harvest, you understand the first important principle: Give! Sow your seed!

But there is another lesson revealed in this parable. That lesson is, when you go forth to sow your seed, be sure that you sow it in fertile ground. God has given you just so much seed to work with. There are many places you can sow that seed. In fact, whether you know it or not, every day you are sowing the seeds that God has entrusted to you — not just your money. There are the seeds of your time. Where are you investing your spare time? Do you invest it in Bible study, worship, Gospel teaching, fellowship in God's name? Or has your time, lately, been too consumed with television, your job, your hobby?

There are the seeds of your love and commitment. We should be sowing those seeds every day, investing our love and our commitment first in God the Father, Christ Jesus and in the Holy Ghost. The next ground where our seeds of commitment should be sown is in the bosom of our families. If you haven't been sowing the seeds of your loyalty in those two places then the seeds haven't been landing in fertile ground.

Finally, there's the seed of your finances, the way you invest the money God has given you. Are you sowing those seeds in fertile ground? You ought to be paying your tithe to your local church and giving the offerings that God lays on your heart. If other endeavors are taking all your money, then you're sowing your seed in the wrong places.

Take an honest look right now at the places where your seed is being sown. Don't be like the sower in the parable who threw most of his seed away on bad ground. Put 100 percent of what you have in the most fertile ground you can find.

The Bible declares,

> Be not deceived; God is not mocked: for whatsoever a man soweth, that shall he also reap. For he that soweth to his flesh shall of the flesh reap corruption; but he that soweth to the Spirit shall of the Spirit reap life everlasting.
>
> And let us not be weary in well doing: for in due season we shall reap, if we faint not"
>
> **Galatians 6:7-9**

If you would reap life everlasting, then sow in the fertile ground of the Spirit.

Take God at His Word! Sow your seed today and watch the blessings of God in return! It has been proven before, and it will be proven in your life if you reach out in faith: *You can't beat God giving!*

Rev. Schambach has personally conducted major open air crusades and meetings in several overseas countries, attracting some of the largest crowds ever assembled in the history of some nations. He preached to 50,000 each night in Georgetown, Guyana, where 25,000 made decisions for Christ and thousands more were healed and delivered through prayer.

Rev. Schambach ministered in Nigeria in 1981, preaching to capacity crowds in four major cities. Two years later, he held four days of services in a government-owned square in Laos, and 25,000 came to Christ.

In 1986, Rev. Schambach conducted a series of meetings throughout the West Indies. Crusades were conducted in Trinidad, Tobago, Grenada, Nevis, St. Kitts, Antigua and Puerto Rico attracting record crowds. In St. Kitts, authorities said the Schambach meeting had a much larger audience than Queen Elizabeth on her visit the previous year.

International Headquarters for Schambach Revivals is located in Tyler, Texas. The ministry provides a 24-hour Power Phone, handling thousands of calls each month from people requesting prayer for salvation, healing or other needs. *Powerline Update* is our monthly publication sent to thousands of partners. Thousands of Rev. Schambach's sermons on video and audio cassettes and in book form are distributed each year.

R. W. Schambach and his wife, Mary Winnifred, were married in 1948. Their three children are actively involved in Schambach Revivals and other Christian ministries.

Schambach Revivals

I truly believe that the ministry of Schambach Revivals represents good ground for seed sowing. For forty years we have been reaching lost souls and bringing deliverance to hurting and broken lives through our "Voice of Power" radio broadcasts. Our tent revivals and crusades have covered North America, leading thousands to Christ and releasing God's power to heal broken bodies and terrible diseases in the lives of thousands. God has called us overseas to be His voice and His messenger to brothers and sisters around the world. Most recently, we presented Gospel crusades in Russia, in places where the name of Jesus had hardly ever been spoken in the past seventy-five years!

This is fertile ground, a place where your seed will ripen and blossom into a harvest of souls for the kingdom of heaven. I invite you to sow your seed here and to learn for yourself that *you can't beat God giving*!

To contact the author,
write:

R. W. Schambach
Schambach Revivals
P. O. Box 9009
Tyler, TX 75711-9009

Other Materials
By
POWER PUBLICATIONS

Books

By R.W. Schambach

You're One In A Million
Power Over Temptation
How To Heal The Sick, Cast Out Devils And Still Go To Hell
Power For Victorious Christian Living
Four Lambs
Miracles: Eyewitness To The Miraculous
You Can't Beat God Givin'
What To Do When Trouble Comes
I Shall Not Want
The Secret Place
After The Fire
The Miracle Manual: *An Evangelism And Prayer Handbook*
The Power Walk Diary
When You Wonder "Why?"
Power Of Faith For Today's Christian
Triumphant Faith
Power Struggle: *Faith For Difficult Relationships*

By Donna Schambach

Tell, Teach & Train

By A.A. Allen

God's Guarantee To Heal You
The Price Of God's Miracle Working Power
Demon Possession Today And How To Be Free

Videos

By R.W. Schambach

Fabulous Fakes: *A Religion Of Form Vs. A Religion Of Force*
Miracles
The Army Of The Lord
How To Raise The Dead
A Life Of Faith
Turn Up The Heat
Don't Touch That Dial
Break The Back Of Debt
Campmeeting With RW Schambach

Cassettes

By R.W. Schambach

(2) Tape Series
Fabulous Fakes: *A Religion Of Form Vs. A Religion Of Force*
The Violent Take It By Force
Power Struggle
After The Fire
Shout

(4) Tape Series
Four Freedoms
A Little Bit Of The Bronx
Fear Not
Classics Of The Faith: *Classic Sermons On Faith & Power*

(6) Tape Series
When You Wonder "Why?"
The Tent Masters

(10) Tape Series
R.W. Schambach's Classic Sermons

By Donna Schambach

(2) Tape Series
How Does Healing Come?
The Dream Team

(3) Tape Series
Revival NOW

For more information about this ministry
and a free product catalog, please write:

SCHAMBACH REVIVALS, INC.
P O BOX 9009
TYLER, TX 75711

To order materials by phone, call
(903)894-6141

WHEN YOU NEED PRAYER

Call the Power Phone

Every day of the week, 24 hours a day, a dedicated, faith-filled, Bible-believing prayer partner is ready to talk with you and pray about your needs. When you need prayer, call:

(903)894-6141

If during the reading of this book, you made a decision to follow Christ, R.W. Schambach has a special gift for you.

He has written a booklet that will help you to continue growing in your new walk with God. It is called, *"You're One In A Million."* And, by simply writing or calling the ministry of Schambach Revivals and letting us know of your decision, we will mail this booklet to you, free of charge.

Write or call: Schambach Revivals
PO Box 9009
Tyler, TX 75711
(903)894-6141